LIONS OF AFRICA

TRACE TAYLOR

SOMEWHERE IN AFRICA, THERE ARE LIONS...

I can see the **lion**.

 **2** I can see the **eye**.

I can see the **mouth**.  3

 I can see the **teeth**.

I can see the **tongue**.

 I can see the **paws**.

I can see the **claws.**  7

 **8** I can see the **pads**.

I can see the **tail**.

 **10** I can see the **baby**.

I can see the **butterfly.**

WHERE LIONS LIVE

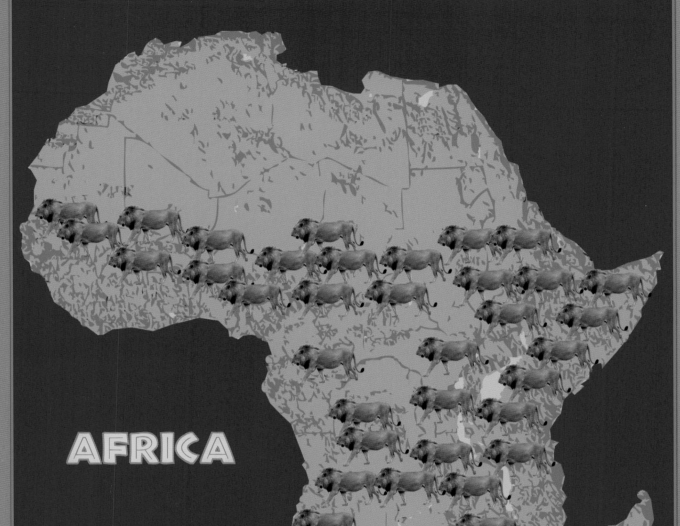

AFRICA

12

MORE ABOUT THE LION...

13

Lions are sneaky hunters. They hide in the tall grass and ambush grazing herd animals. They even separate into two groups. One group waits in the grass, while the other group chases the animals right into the waiting group's claws. Working as a team, these big cats keep the family fed.

The lion's typical meal consists of zebra, buffalo, wildebeest, or antelope. They normally avoid big, dangerous game, but when starving, they will hunt grown elephants and giraffes.

Jackals are scavengers that wait on the heels of feeding lions. When the lions finish eating, jackals move in and eat anything the lions have left behind. Jackals also hunt small game that the lions ignore, like rabbits, rats, and sometimes young lion cubs.

Vultures are large birds that scour the plains for carcasses and fresh kills. These birds find the kills and steal nibbles whenever possible. Once the lions are gone, the vultures stay to eat anything that is left.

A male lion wins the ownership of a pride by defeating the older male in battle. Male lions are caring and affectionate to the cubs of their pride. They keep them safe from predators and male lions from other prides.

The female lions of a pride usually give birth around the same time of year as each other. They nurse and care for all the cubs of the pride, not just their own. So all the cubs have lots of food, protection, and care.

I can match the words to the pictures using the first letter sounds.

claws

mouth

pads

tongue

POWER WORDS

How many can you read?

I

can

see

the

21

1-3Y: Skills Card

Reader: _____   Room: _____

"What was this book mainly about? How do you know?"

1Y	Listen to and remember the sentence pattern in Yellow books. Use the pattern and pictures to read the rest of the book.

2Y	Point to each word as I read. Use the spaces to separate words.
	Try again if what I say doesn't match the number of words.

3Y	Make the sound of the first letter of the new word on the page, check the picture, then say something that matches both.

I can get my mouth ready for:

b	c	d
f	g	h
j	k	l
m	n	p
r	s	t
v	w	z